My Hands

By Lloyd G. Douglas

Children's Press®
A Division of Scholastic Inc.
New York / Toronto / London / Auckland / Sydney
Mexico City / New Delhi / Hong Kong
Danbury, Connecticut

Photo Credits: Cover © Anthony Nex/Corbis; p. 5 © Roderick Chen/SuperStock, Inc.; p. 7 © Tom & Dee Ann McCarthy/Corbis; pp. 9, 21 (top left) © Will & Deni McIntyre/Corbis; pp. 11, 21 (top right) © GoodShot/SuperStock, Inc.; pp. 13, 17, 21 (bottom right) © Corbis; pp. 15, 21 (bottom left) © Strauss/Curtis/Corbis; p. 19 © Ariel Skelley/Corbis
Contributing Editor: Shira Laskin
Book Design: Michael de Guzman

Library of Congress Cataloging-in-Publication Data

Douglas, Lloyd G.
    My hands / by Lloyd G. Douglas.
    p. cm.—(My body)
    Summary: Simple text introduces the functions of the human hand, as well as tools that can help people who have no hands.
    Includes bibliographical references.
    ISBN 0-516-24059-5 (lib. bdg.)—ISBN 0-516-22128-0 (pbk.)
    1. Hand—Juvenile literature. [1. Hand. 2. Human anatomy.] I. Title. II. Series.

QM548.D68 2004
612'.97—dc22

               2003012004

Contents

I have two hands.

I have five **fingers** on
each hand.

One of my fingers is called a **thumb**.

My thumb helps me
hold things.

I can hold a pencil.

9

We use our fingers to touch things.

We can feel things that are soft.

Most people are **right-handed**.

They use their right hand to write and to do many other things.

Some people are **left-handed**.

They use their left hand to do most things.

15

People use their hands to do many things.

Some people play musical **instruments** with their hands.

Some people do not have hands.

They use special **tools** to hold and move things.

19

Our hands are very **useful** parts of our bodies.

21

New Words

fingers (**fing**-guhrz) the five body parts at the end of the hand

instruments (in-**struh**-muhnts) things used to make music

left-handed (**left**-**hand**-id) being able to use the left hand more easily than the right

right-handed (**rite**-**hand**-id) being able to use the right hand more easily than the left

thumb (**thuhm**) the short, thick first finger on the hand

tools (**toolz**) something that helps you do a special job

useful (**yooss**-fuhl) something that is helpful and can be used a lot

To Find Out More

Books

My Fingers Are for Touching
by Jane Belk Moncure
The Child's World, Inc.

My Hands
by Aliki
HarperCollins Children's Book Group

Web Site
Touching
www.fi.edu/qa97/me10/me10.html
Read about the sense of touch, learn experiments to
do with your sense of touch, and learn about different
touch types on this Web site.

Index

About the Author
Lloyd G. Douglas has written many books for children.

Reading Consultants
Kris Flynn, Coordinator, Small School District Literacy, The San Diego County Office of Education

Shelly Forys, Certified Reading Recovery Specialist, W.J. Zahnow Elementary School, Waterloo, IL

Paulette Mansell, Certified Reading Recovery Specialist, and Early Literacy Consultant, TX

24